I0412215

Hello, my name is Jamie Valencia Wilkinson (Wilkinson-Watson) and I am the proud, married mother of two beautiful children.

My brand new book is entitled, "How To Make Yourself Happy"-- please enjoy!

Throughout the years, humans have struggled to survive their everyday stresses and stressors.

Each day people seem to be overwhelmed by their "problems" and simply do not know what to do.

Within my book, I will try to cover some possible ways (in no particular order) to help relief you of your everyday burdens and find comfort within.

Always remember the state of happiness is a choice-- one must choose to be happy despite their circumstance(s).

Let Go Of The Past

Sometimes, this is easier said than done. I think if the source of your guilt comes from your past, you must first identify it, let it go, then move on.

You should tell yourself that if there is nothing reminding you of it then move on-- that was the old you. Be the bigger person and own up to it while remembering that you are no longer that person! If you want to continue to be that person then thats where you go wrong.

<u>Take A Deep Breath</u>

When people try to mess you up or stress you out, stay calm and take a deep breath of fresh air. Breathing in will allow your brain to receive the oxygen that it needs for your body to operate in healthy manner-- you will be able to think clear thoughts and just get over the pettiness that is aimed toward you.

Count To Ten

If the person or persons; situation or situations are just too much for you, you could try counting to ten. Doing so would allow you both the time to think and calm down simultaneously.

<u>Find Something To Smile About</u>

If you find yourself feeling bored, and down take a few minutes to smile. You can look at pictures of family or a vacation, speak with your kids and grand kids (and other family members), etc

Watch A Comedy

During the morning or the evening, sit back and watch a good comedy. Nothing is better than enjoying hours of laughter.

This laughter is literally medicine for your body and soul. You will definitely feel better!

<u>Go On A Vacation</u>

Visit the caribbean or just take time off from work to enjoy your life. Planning a vacation should be an occassion to unwind and relax from your hectic schedule.

A good place to visit is The Bahamas. Please read my guide, *A Guide On Visiting The Bahamas*, available on Amazon and Createspace.

<u>Eat A Balanced Meal</u>

Very often, we feel bad because we lack a balanced meal. Prepare a nice colorful plate and drink at least one glass of water afterward.

Once, you get the adequate vitamins and minerals needed, your body knows it and responds-- you actually feel better!

Go For A Jog

Whenever you have the chance, go for a jog. It improves breathing, blood circulation and your heart beat.

Purchase Something For Someone

Nothing feels better than buying a gift for someone-- it doesn't have to be expensive. What matters the most is that you saw the need to help someone out and you did!

Go Shopping for Yourself

Every so often, you need a "pick me up". Budget a few hundred dollars and buy yourself something special.

I can almost guarantee that just looking at your purchases at the end of the day is bound to give you some form of gratification!

Go For A Swim

If you can swim, go to the beach or your pool and take a nice swim! If you can't then just stand in the shallow part and relax.

<u>Sleep</u>

Many times, you may feel cranky because you did not have sufficient sleep. In psychology there is something called the "circadian cycle" .

Everyone has to get a certain amount of sleep in order to function properly throughout the day or night.

<u>Drink Lots Of Water</u>

Drinking water helps the blood to circulate properly, helps digestion and filters the blood of harmful toxins.

It is usually suggested that an individual drink eight glasses of water a day.

Cleanse Your Body

You can rid your body of impurities in a number of ways. One drink lots of water, two eat fruits and vegetables and three sweat it out.

Massage

Life is hard. Treat yourself to a nice massage. This would help you to get rid of unwanted kinks and other pains.You would walk away feeling renewed and rejuvenated.

<u>Take A Hot Shower</u>

Take a hot shower and melt away pains like headaches and cramps. It is also a good idea to soak your feet in a bucket of hot water. You can actually feel the blood rush while it is circulating.

<u>Set Goals For Yourself</u>

One of the best things you can do for yourself is to set goals-- whether long term or short term.

Examples of long term would be to save up for a new car. And an example of a short term goal would be to lose one dress or pant(s) size.

<u>Listen To Music</u>

Choose a genre of music that you like and create a playlist of your favorite songs-- for free of course. Then lay back on your couch or bed and enjoy hours and hours of it.

Paint Or Draw A Picture

Spend some time being an artist. Try to paint a picture of the ocean, the park or a town. Sometimes, you can auction your artwork off for money online-- you never know what potential you have until you put your paintings (and other art) out there.

<u>Create A Garden</u>

Plant flowers and fruit trees with your free time. Nothing will make you more happier than seeing your seedlings grow.

You would improve your environment and the ecosystems that exist around you.

Conclusion

Only you can make you happy. Do not let others steal your inner peace and joy. You are an individual and you deserve the best in this life!

Whenever you have a problem try to eleviate that nuisance. Challenges never go away unless you address them the best way you know how.

Have a good life-- the best one you that only you can have!

Helpful Resources

www.helpguide.org/mental/stress_management_relief_coping.htm

www.mayoclinic.com/health/stress-management/MY00435

http://visitingthebahamas.intuitwebsites.com/

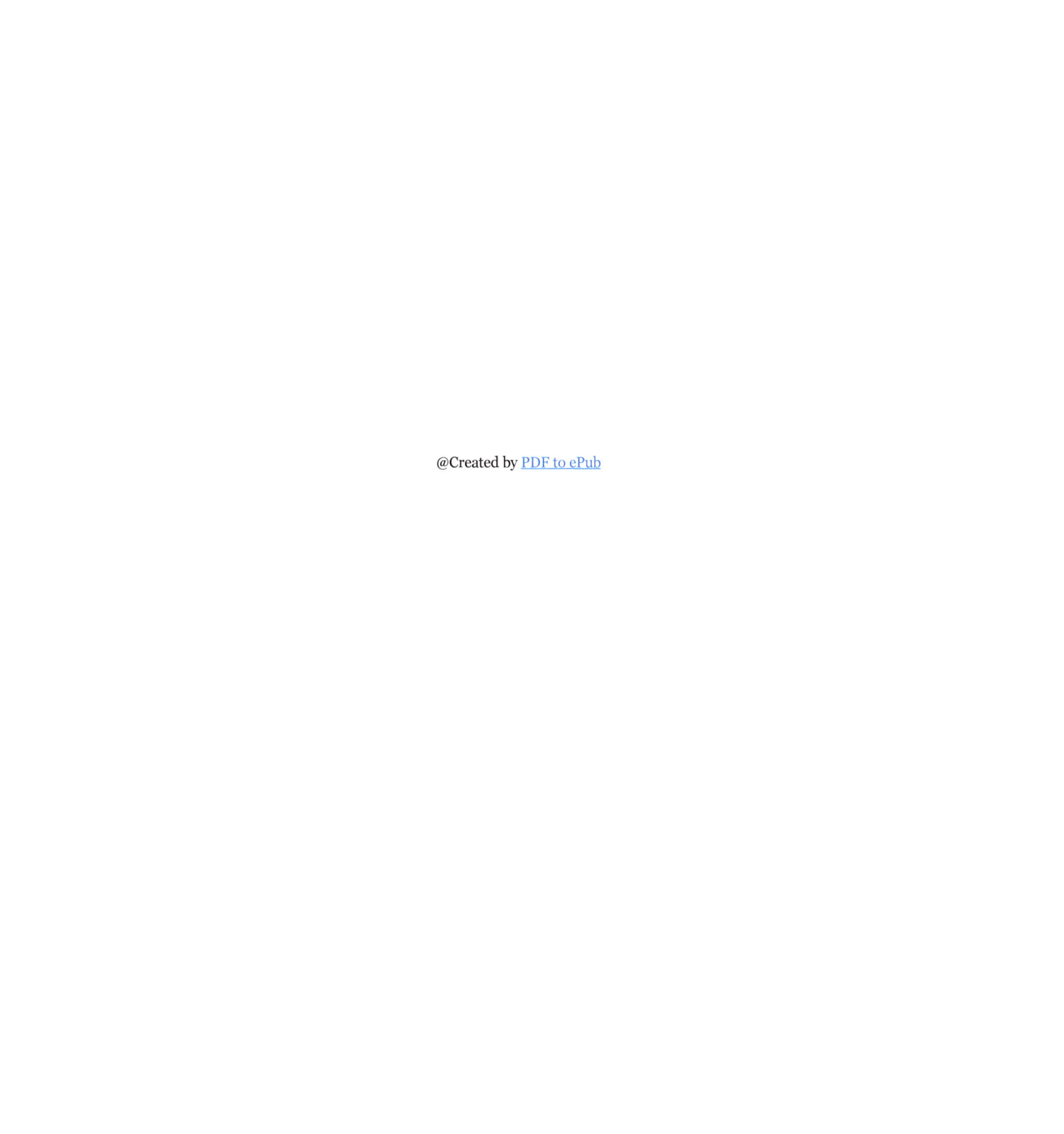

@Created by [PDF to ePub](#)

www.ingramcontent.com/pod-product-compliance
Lightning Source LLC
Chambersburg PA
CBHW060822290526

45792CB00005BB/1767